102

HAIKU

JOURNAL

17 Syllables to Say It All

ABRAMS NOTERIE, NEW YORK

Design by Hana Nakamura

ISBN 978-1-4197-2677-4

Printed and bound in China
10 9 8 7 6 5 4 3 2 1

Abrams Noterie products are available at special
discounts when purchased in quantity for premiums
and promotions as well as fundraising or educational
use. Special editions can also be created to specification.
For details, contact specialsales@abramsbooks.com or
the address below.

ABRAMS The Art of Books
115 West 18th Street, New York, NY 10011
abramsbooks.com

a human being
is the owner of this fine
book of haiku thoughts

INTRODUCTION

Welcome to your new mission.

It's clear that you are the type of person who is interested in living a life that is an adventure, whatever that adventure may be. You want to do and see great things.

We know that every great thing we want to see in the world has got to start with the only great thing that we truly control.

The great thing that you see every morning when you look in the mirror.

You.

When it comes to the power of haiku to learn about yourself, we are the experts. We write custom poems for strangers every day, all around the world; it is an intimate and revelatory experience.

Our mission is to inspire people to take bold action in the pursuit of passion. It looks like you are on that mission now, too.

We're on this mission together.

Q: What Is a Haiku Anyway?
A: An Unusual Strophe

As we delve into the world of haiku together, let's note our context: We are English-speaking Westerners who have studied poetic forms spanning linguistic, historic, and cultural divides. We've taken haiku out of its original context of ancient Japanese culture and are experimenting with it for contemporary Western audiences. We do so with the utmost respect for the original art form and all of our knowledge and guidance has the purpose of bringing haiku into a new time and place, never to tell any traditional Japanese artists how they should write haiku.

Many people remember haiku from early grade school—what a great opportunity for our teachers to show us what syllables are. But some people must have been absent during that day of second grade; we'll never forget the day an angry fellow stormed over to our haiku stand demanding to know, "WHAT IS A HACKUS?!?"

In the English-speaking world, the classic definition of a haiku is any three-line poem, with a syllabic structure of 5-7-5. There is a lot more going on in the traditional Japanese style. There are two crucial elements of the traditional Japanese haiku: a *kireji* (cutting word) between two different thoughts or images, and a *kigo* (seasonal reference). These rules are often set aside in the construction of Western-style haiku, and we're cool with that, but it is important to at least know that in Japanese, the syllable "hai" means "unusual" and "ku" means "strophe" or "verse." So the word *haiku* translates exactly to an "unusual strophe." That definition is pretty important in the application of haiku to our daily lives because every haiku is an opportunity for a fresh perspective.

Haiku started to emerge in ancient Japan nearly 1,000 years ago, as a casual, collaborative poetic form. It wasn't until the time of the great master Matsuo Basho (1644–1694) that the *hokku*, the standalone 5-7-5 poem, reached real greatness and prestige as more than just a witty party trick.

Basho was the first in a new line of masterful haiku poets who revolutionized cultural life in Japan, and his followers became the leaders of generations of haiku masters like Buson, Issa, Shiki, and rarer, though prolific, women haikuists like Chigetsu, Kikusha, and Chiyo. As soon as Western writers heard of this beautiful poetic form, it gained traction and attention worldwide. Foreign people living in Japan and internationally minded Japanese and experimental writers interested in minimalism all caught wind of the magic of haiku.

And now we are here.

Don't you think it's time to start?

Are you ready yet?

(See what we did there?)

HOW TO HAIKU

There Must Be 50 Ways to Write Your Haiku

Over the course of this book you're going to be struck by inspiration in many different ways. Like all things, writing haiku gets easier with practice, we swear. Until the ideas start flowing like water, try some of these exercises to get your muses talking to you.

Or, if you're ready, skip ahead to start your haiku adventure.

Exercise 1: Think about your life.

Make a list of ten or more words or phrases that describe you, your passions, your dreams, challenges in your life, and things you love. Be as specific as possible. And it doesn't need to sound "poetic"—this is just a freely associated list for you and you will not need to turn it in to the teacher.

Exercise 2: Visualization.

Close your eyes and take a few slow,
deep breaths, as calmly as possible.
Give yourself about sixty seconds of
uninterrupted quiet breath. You'll
start to notice images arising in
your head. Let your mind wander
to scenes, pictures, and scenarios
that you enjoy—scenes of nature,
certain sounds, colors, scents, tastes,
textures. After a few minutes of
meandering in that mindscape, start
listing as many of these sensory
words and descriptors as you can.
They don't need to connect or make
sense, just let your mind go off on its
own and see what you find.

Exercise 3: Synthesis.

The most powerful way to inspire
is to connect a powerful image
or metaphor with an idea that is
meaningful to you. Look at your lists
and start to imagine connection
between your life and the sensory
exploration you did. You'll probably
find a connection that is really
strong and hits you fast. If not, start
pairing things arbitrarily and see
what you get.

Exercise 4:
Refinement and calibration.

The beauty of a haiku, or any poem
really, is in the way phrases can
feel new and fresh with just small
tweaks from how you'd normally
talk. Try writing a full sentence
about something on your mind.
Now look closely at it and pull it
apart. You can move all the sections
around, reverse the order, go back
and forth from passive and active
voice, change perspective, make
it sound like Yoda said it, and it
doesn't even need to "make sense";
think of it like magnetic poetry.

Exercise 5:
New writing implements.

We get inspired just by using a
typewriter—the experience is so
different than typing on a computer
or chicken scratch in one of our
tattered notebooks. You can inspire
yourself too, just by using a writing
tool you don't usually use. Felt tip
marker, mechanical pencil, nail
polish, India ink, calligraphy pen,
old lipstick. . . just don't blame us if
things get messy. Or do, if it will get
you out of trouble.

YOUR HAIKU

THE HAIKU
PROMPTS

it's with gratitude
and with no further adieu
we start to haiku

1

Your First Memory

Childhood was a big Crayola blur for many of us, but what was one formative moment that stands out in your mind? Crawling across your grandma's shag carpet? Eating glitter in preschool? Your older brother throwing a walnut at your head? Look back and put yourself in that moment, and enjoy the simplicity and strangeness of the world through your childhood eyes.

it was so shiny
I'd never have imagined
it would taste so bad

DATE: ___ • ___ • ___

2

Your First View of a New World

Imagine you were raised in a bunker seventeen feet beneath the earth's crust. Finally, one glorious day, you climb out and see the sky for the first time, feel the sun and wind, hear the birds. . .what are birds anyway? What seventeen syllables can encapsulate that feeling?

*Going outside on a bright day can help with this one.

my skin caught on fire
the white above me blinding
singing foreign songs

Haiku for the Sun

When people ask us for haiku, often they learn something new about themselves, just by thinking of a haiku topic. Searching for poetic themes, you can stumble across interesting preferences, one of which is for either sunrise or sunset. Some people are all about the former, and others are moved to tears by the latter. Which do you prefer, and why? Hash it out in a haiku.

never satisfied
always playing tricks with us
spinning us 'round you

Unmentionables

Would you ever write a poem about your underwear? Probably not, but why not write about the feeling you get from something you wear (almost) every day. How does it feel to the touch? Should it have a certain presentation? And what about all those other things that come with it like the putting on and the taking off, flinging them around, etc. Pick something you want to say about your underwear and write a haiku about it.

just cuz I'm thirty
doesn't mean it's not okay
as the bat signal

DATE: ___ • ___ • ___

Walking Haiku

Put your phone down. Put your shoes on. Go out walking right now for at least twenty minutes—who knows, maybe you'll wander for longer—with no destination or distractions. You can bring a small notebook to write observations if you like, or go with nothing at all. When you return, write a haiku about something that you observed or something that happened on your adventure.

easier with breeze
river passing by the trees
forgetting all else

6

No Rules, Just Rights

You know when you were a kid and some authority figure told you something you had to do, or something you were forbidden to do, and that arbitrary rule totally baffled you? Have you ever looked back and realized that some of those rules were absolutely vital to your survival? What was one rule you have a new appreciation for?

flow of traffic slows
when a child runs up the down
staircase with no rail

The Best of Friends

You and your best friend love one another unconditionally. But they probably have a habit of doing something a certain way that just annoys the crap out of you. Maybe you've communicated this aggravation, or maybe you haven't. Either way, you've learned to deal with it (hopefully). Further commemorate that quirk by writing a haiku about it and make plans to deliver it today. Extra points if you tell them to write one about your quirky and/or obnoxious trait.

before you say no
for arbitrary reasons—
let's give it a shot

DATE: ___ • ___ • ___

8

Attitude of Gratitude

We're not telling you to be grateful, but we are telling you it feels really good. Today, who deserves your utmost gratitude, appreciation, and compassion? You have a lot to give, so dish it out right here, to that special person who needs it.

*Bonus if you tell them— they'll love it.

nearest and dearest
dogliest dogs beside me
all for one for all

DATE: ___ • ___ • ___

How to Haiku Your Last Meal

The perfect aerial shot of a beautiful meal can feel almost poetic, right? Write a haiku to describe your last memorable meal, but instead of talking about it like plain old food, describe your meal like it was an epic action sequence or passionate love scene.

covered in crimson
sea of slithering serpents
meaty bombs away

DATE: ___ • ___ • ___

10

Haiku for Connection

What makes you feel most connected to others or the world around you?

the door almost slams
in my face—but a stranger
grabs it right in time

DATE: ___ • ___ • ___

11

Math Haiku—The Pythagorean Theorem

Pythagoras and his crew discovered that to find the length of the hypotenuse of a right triangle, you only had to find the square root of the sum of the squares of the other two sides. Write a haiku where the third line is a solution to sum of the first two.

A squared + B squared = C squared

where to get started?
all these options look equal
. . .till you get closer

12

A Tree of Haiku

Who doesn't love looking at and appreciating a tree? But, what does the tree see, looking back at all of humanity? We leave this question in your hands.

googley eyeballs
sticking on potato sacks
never can sit still

13

Reach for Great Depth

Depth explores the age-old idea that one cannot judge a book by its cover. There is always something deeper lying beneath the surface, ready to be explored, or maybe even hiding and waiting to be found. What does depth mean to you?

our images can
never surmise the power
behind each our eyes

14.

Your Least Favorite Good Habit

You have many habits you've developed that have a positive impact on your life. You do these things daily and for the betterment of your livelihood. But there is a "but": Deep down, you really don't enjoy doing them. Pick one of these habits and tell it like it is.

rinsing with mouthwash
both before and after brush
takes up twice the time

15

Your Most Favorite Bad Habit

All this thinking about good habits made us think of the bad habits we share. Ponder one of your favorite bad habits that you partake in from time to time, indulge yourself in a haiku about it.

so many dear friends
met whence puffing death closer
outside for fresh air

_____

_____

_____

16

Tidy Up the Fridge

Rotting food, weird smells, slimy leftovers. A clean and glorious refrigerator will make you feel great, encourage you to buy healthy vibrant food, and make your roommates LOVE YOU FOREVER. When you get a chance, tidy up the fridge and write a haiku about it. If the haiku inspires you, hang it up on the fridge, where it belongs.

frostbitten peas fell
out of the freezer today—
nobody wants them

Say Something
By Saying Nothing

Sometimes a way to say
something is by just not saying
anything at all. Write about
silence as a statement.

I would describe it
but instead I bring your eyes
to see for themselves

_____

_____

_____

DATE: ___ • ___ • ___

18

Motherhood: A Haiku

Write a haiku today about either your mom, your favorite maternal figure, or whatever motherhood may mean to you. It need not sound like a greeting card—go with your gut.

I hope that someday
I'll be able to tell you
and you'll understand

19

Love Something You Hate

Write a haiku for your least favorite word or thing as if it were your favorite. This is more than just silver linings, this is trying to seek out a genuine love nugget for something you may have never given any appreciation. If you can do this, you can literally do ANYTHING. So give it a shot.

traffic ain't so bad
when we're in it together
it's quality time

20

Haiku for Yesterday

Write yourself a note forgiving
yourself for one thing you didn't
love about yesterday.

passive aggressive
emails easily erased
with morning bagels

DATE: ___ • ___ • ___

21

That Thing You Meant To Do...

What's something you've pretty much given up on? Something you would have liked to stick to longer? Commemorate that thing in haiku form, and ask yourself if you want to give it another shot. If you don't want to give it another shot, that's fine, too.

Japanese lessons
seemed like such a good idea
before I started

DATE: ___ • ___ • ___

22

Mindfulness

What is your zen? How do you feel when you are physically and mentally relaxed? Try out this practice for a mindful haiku. Sit or lie in a comfortable position and take stock of how you feel, mentally and physically. Next, for ten breaths, inhale and exhale through your nose at a natural pace. Focus all your attention on your breath. After you're done, gently notice how your body and mind feel. What are your sensations? What, if anything, has changed?

my heart, burning sun
gradually sinks beneath
the breath's horizon

_____

_____

_____

DATE: ___ • ___ • ___

23

Hear the Sounds
Your Body Makes

Like it or not, your body is an
instrument that sometimes
produces rhythms not just for
your ears alone. There are so
many sounds but you can only
pick one—the one that first comes
to mind. Describe the musical
process involved, just don't give
it away.

chewing sounds louder
when it's done with your mouth closed—
drown boring small talk

24.

The Voice of Reason

Poetry can be fun, of course, but it is also said to be the voice of reason, the voice of pain and struggle. For generations it has telegraphed the human condition, recording injustice and issues of the times. There are many forms of unfortunate truths facing our society today, why not take a shot at explaining one that has been bothering you lately.

united we stand
colorblind because we know
divided we fall

DATE: ___ • ___ • ___

25

Love Is the Feeling

The topic of "love" emerges again
and again throughout our lives,
in so many different ways. It just
might be the biggest and most
complex haiku topic in the world.
Are you in love? Looking for love?
Feeling love for the universe?
Questioning the meaning of love?
What does love mean to you,
right at this very moment?

swelling up inside
I forget to take a breath
inhale, exhale, smile

DATE: ___ • ___ • ___

26

Haiku Is the Lord of the Dance

Music can set free a part of you that you never knew existed: a part of you that loves to dance. Even if you don't consider yourself to be much of a dancer, everybody has a jam that makes them feel that special feeling, that deep down, grooving they can't help but move to. Find that song, turn up the volume, and dance with all your might. Try a new move, get awkward. Do anything you want. Now, write about it.

wigglin' jiggle
open-up-shop pop-n-drop
slow-mo no-fomo

DATE: ___ • ___ • ___

27

Long Words, Short Poems

We always think of haiku in syllables. But what about looking at the actual number of words? Try to write a haiku with the least words possible. Five words is a challenge—what about even fewer?

unfortunately
depravity's clauses were
aerodynamic

28

A Serendipitous Commute

We go to school or work the same way almost every day. What would happen if we decided to give ourselves a bit of extra time to see what else the world has in store for us this morning or this evening? Veer off your quotidian pathway and open up some space for serendipity in your day. Tell us what happens the short and sweet way.

bike stayed chained today
and a police officer
said he liked my shoes

29

The Secret Is Out

We all have secrets. Some (okay, most) we would not tell a stranger during small talk. What would catch them off guard if you were to share? Haiku it and do it.

that booger dangles
with an iron grip upon
outermost nose hair

30

Haiku for Today

Something happened today, be it big or small. What was it?

I spit my gum out
but it missed the trashcan just
as you watched it fly

31

Gender

It can be easy to take gender for granted, but walking a mile in someone else's shoes can shed light on our own identity. Imagine you're a different gender. What does it feel like? How are your thoughts different? Try to look at your gender in a new way for this haiku.

*Bonus if you share this with someone who identifies as that gender and get their opinion.

it was so easy
that I didn't even know
how easy it was

32

Hometown Haiku

Everyone has a special
association with their hometown.
Whether you've moved away
and are homesick, still live in
the house where you grew up, or
ran away and never looked back,
address the place of your birth in
a haiku—good, bad, or both.

bedroom still intact
but some of my favorite
restaurants are gone

33

The Worldly Wordsmith and the Armchair Traveler

Haiku can be written in any language, and from any place on earth. Think of a place you'd like to visit, where the national language is not English, and write a haiku about that place. Now, use a translating app, dictionary, or real live human to translate it to that language. Write about what makes it unique or just some things that come to mind. This is your chance to not worry about syllables in your final haiku.

池;水の音
そして、星が見事に上昇します
それぞれで、山富士

pond; sound of water
and stars rising brilliantly
in each, Mt. Fuji

DATE: ___ • ___ • ___

The Most Boring Haiku in the World

The magic of haiku is the way that it can make even the most mundane, average things seem fresh. Conjure up an activity you do every day. Now, write a haiku that makes that banal action into a magical fantasy vignette.

I would tie my shoe
but I am a snake charmer
so they loop themselves

DATE: ___ • ___ • ___

35

A Life in Trinkets

Sitting down to write, especially when it's been a while, can feel pretty intimidating. But did you know you've got an entire treasure chest of inspiration (or at least a few distinct pieces of inspiration) with you right now? Reach into your pocket, purse, backpack, briefcase or top hat and take out a few objects. Now pick an object (or two) and create a haiku.

*Bonus points if you can connect two objects that seemingly have nothing in common!

an empty gift card
hugs the melted lip balm, lies,
says they will be spared

DATE: ___ • ___ • ___

36

How Infinite Everything Can Be...

What does ∞ mean to you?
Tell yourself in a haiku.

choosing the amount
of "what ifs" you will let be
always unanswered

DATE: ___ • ___ • ___

35

Life Is a Ladder

There is a timeless argument about who has been hurt or oppressed more, as if winning that argument will change or help anything. What if we gave that up and just lifted each other?

won the gold medal
and the crowd goes wild cheering—
we ran together

38

The Haiku Chef

The art of making and sharing food is beautiful and very worthwhile. Look in your kitchen and fix up a meal for one, two, or more. Instead of using a recipe, make something new and spontaneous. Write about it after.

it was movie time—
kernels tossed in bacon grease
barely needed salt

DATE: ___ • ___ • ___

39

Intuition Is Inside

We are told to follow "the rules" all of the time. What if the world had no rules, what would you follow then? How would you know what action to take if you had to create your own path with no one judging you or pressuring you to act in a certain, acceptable way? Intuition is our inner voice of clarity, the thing that is deeper than the rules of society. Write yourself a haiku that taps into that voice, that little Jiminy Cricket within.

grounded to the floor
close my eyes to clearly see
no hesitation

Haiku for Tomorrow

Write yourself a note about how amazing tomorrow will be.

even my coffee
will taste more sweet and creamy
no need for sugar

DATE: ___ • ___ • ___

4·1

Haiku Your Fortune

We all know the pleasure of cracking apart a fortune cookie and discovering the message inside. Whether profound, absurd, or even nonsensical, it's a secret surprise just for you. What bite-sized advice would you give, or what future would you forecast inside a fortune cookie of your own?

the greatest sweetness
comes not in spoonfuls or lumps
but savored moments

For a Long Lost Friend or Relative

Who have you lost touch with, for no reason at all? Life gets in the way sometimes, but we can get ahead of it by reaching back out to people who are meaningful to us. Write a haiku for someone you haven't talked to in ages—and why not send it to them?

remember when we
talked on the phone till sunrise
and met for breakfast?

4.3

Haiku-pedia

Maybe you've never donated the $5/year that Wikipedia begs of you to sustain itself and provide free knowledge to the entire planet, but you've definitely used it as a resource to learn about things foreign to you. Go to Wikipedia, click "bring me to a random page," take the time to actually read it, and write a haiku about it. One million extra points if you donate to Wikipedia afterward.

The Wiki page we visited: Union Square (Somerville).

curious indeed
that the Red Sox are not called
the Yankees instead

Who Runs the World? Haiku

A lot of people vie for the opportunity, but it must be pretty hard to be a world leader. We get asked to write about presidents, political figures, and news-making controversial characters all the time—who do you think should have a haiku dedicated to them, and what should it say?

*Bonus if you tweet their haiku at them with #freehaiku.

when the president
hires haiku flight attendants—
Airforce Seventeen

_____

_____

_____

DATE: ___ • ___ • ___

Haiku Alliteration—Harder Than It Sounds, Literally

The tools of rhetoric are many. One of our favorite, and one of the simplest, is alliteration. All you have to do is chose a letter, and make every single word in this haiku start with that letter. (Technically it's called consonance if you use a consonant and alliteration if you use a vowel—follow your heart.)

*Bonus if it makes sense.

dearly do dreamers
dandelion diligent
dire deliveries

Haiku for Mad Men

We see ads all day every day, even when we don't notice them. Look out for an interesting print ad or billboard today and turn it into a haiku.

*Bonus if you send it to the company and tell them what's up.

real estate agents
why are all your orange heads
floating o'er our homes?

Observation Deck

Read this haiku prompt in the
morning, then wait to write until
evening. Choose one thing now
that you want to observe all day.
It can be something omnipresent
like the sun, another being like
your dog, or your own experience,
like how your ears feel. Be more
aware of this one thing and
jot down some notes. Tonight,
write a haiku about what you've
discovered.

an ocean of frowns
every debbie and oscar
hiding happiness

The Gold Gilding of the Memory of a Kiss

A kiss. Just one kiss. And one haiku to put it down in history. You are Gustav Klimt and this is your "The Kiss."

imperceptibly—
the breath of space between us
flew between our lips

Upstream or Downstream?

Imagine you're out hiking and come to a stream. Do you feel inclined to follow it upstream to find its source, or downstream to see where it leads? Haiku that instinct.

you and I both know
this water comes from somewhere
one clue where it goes

50

GOOOOOALS

You're probably working toward
something in your life, or at least
thinking about it. What is it?

count twenty-six miles
how many footsteps is that?
road rise to meet me

DATE: ___ • ___ • ___

51

Hidden Worlds

Children love to populate their world with fantastic companions. When we grow older, we often forget to fill the spaces between our houseplants with tiny footprints, or feel too self-conscious to think how great a ride on a dragonfly might be if you were the right size. Take a moment to revert to being an open-eyed kid and imagine what in your environment might make a good home for a faerie.

at the bird feeder
one hummingbird's a bit slow—
might be the saddle

52

The Saddest Haiku in This Whole Book

Sometimes it's okay to just let yourself get a little teary-eyed. Usually we let romance films do it, but you have the power to make yourself misty. Write the saddest haiku you could ever imagine—write something that makes you want to cry.

would it might have been—
but forlorn hopeless bones broke
while we were asleep

53

Soaping It Up

Do you use bar soap? Or shower gel? A loofa? Or just your hands? Maybe you use free range sea sponges and sea salt lavender scrubs, or maybe you can't remember the last time you needed more than water to do the trick. Write about your soap experience.

cedarwood lather
bar slipping out of my hand
it lasts just two weeks

DATE: ___ • ___ • ___

54

Gone Awry

When everything goes wrong. . .
you close your eyes and go to a
safe place. Describe it in a haiku.

a baby deer smiles
and brings me a scotch mallow
in this green meadow

DATE: ___ • ___ • ___

55

Mountains Out of Mole Hills

We exist in a world where we take for granted the scale of the things around us. Ants are so small you can hardly see them. Redwood trees tower over us. But what if we could work a bit of magic on our surroundings and choose one tiny thing to make enormous? What miniscule creature would you expand, and how big?

a blade of grass casts
shadow that blocks out the sun
pebbles, now mountains

_____

_____

_____

DATE: ___ • ___ • ___

56

A Meta Moment

Write a haiku about haiku writing.

slaving syllables
plagiarizing nature's tales
trying not to count

You Are a Cloud

You are a cloud. What is the sky? What is sound? What is texture and light? What do you witness from above the earth? What does the earth see above it?

slopes of Mt. Fuji
cooled by such a subtle hand—
millions of fingers

58

Poetic Review

We love to write reviews of movies, plays, books, and art in haiku form because the haiku helps us get to the heart of the matter. Haiku can also be a refreshing way to process other longer forms of poetry. Choose a poem and review it in haiku form. The challenge is to retain some of the tone, a reference to the content, and incorporate your own take, all in three lines—are you up for it?

For Lin-Manuel Miranda's *Hamilton*

do not miss your shot
this will only occur once
as the candle burns

DATE: ___ • ___ • ___

59

Refugee Haiku

You may never want to leave
this place you call home, still the
choice can be taken from you, as
is the case for many refugees
in the world today. Express the
feeling of a forced departure from
the place you have come to love.

bye to the pillow
that held up my head last night—
I cannot carry

60

Haiku for Jealousy

What are you jealous of? Think about what makes you green with envy.

next table over
their conversation must be
so flapping funny

61

Fight for What You Care About

So much of what is happening in the world at any given time can really suck the happiness right out of you. We have global warming, terrorism, poverty, and endless reasons to be alarmed. Lisa Borden said that if you're not outraged, then you're just not paying attention. Take a moment to grab onto your dissatisfaction, not generally but specifically with the state of one thing in the world right now, and pour it out. Maybe you'll even stumble across a solution.

sometimes when I see
something labeled VIP
I want to smash it

62

Sunrise / Sunset

Your bedroom will face either
east or west, and you have no
curtains. Which do you choose—
the sun rising east or the sun
setting west? Write about one.

*Bonus if you write about both.

going to bed late
so that we can wake up in
early afternoon

63

A Song That Changed Your Life

Music is something that everyone can relate to and shapes our innermost selves. Sometimes a specific song or artist can even change the direction of your life. If you don't believe us, go out and read Bob Boilen's book, *Your Song Changed My Life.* Now's the time to haiku about the amazing power music has over us. Give it a shot—what song changed your life?

A song that changed our lives?
"Title and Registration"
by Death Cab for Cutie.

until I knew you
it was only christian rock—
well, that and enya

64.

The Existential Crisis Haiku

Write a haiku as if you do not yet exist. Boom.

do we remember
the simplicity of earth
before we brought dawn

DATE: ___ • ___ • ___

65

Old as Dirt

What is the oldest thing you own? Do you have some family heirloom, or have you picked up a strange antique along the road? Maybe you're a modernist and the oldest thing you own is younger than you are. Whatever it is, find that ancient thing and describe its epic life.

leather once was plush
now the zipper is broken
grandpa's travel bag

DATE: ___ • ___ • ___

66

Because You're Worth It

What is the last thing you bought yourself? Write a haiku about that unique feeling of treating yourself.

crown deserves temple
regalia rewarded
for hiding bed head

_____

_____

_____

DATE: ___ • ___ • ___

67

The Elephant in the Room

Keep an eye out today for
something that is totally
out of place—physically or
metaphorically. Write a haiku
for its awkward or interesting
situation. Life's funny that way.

garbage piled high
above the top of the can
no one takes it out

68

Your Favorite Spot

Everyone has somewhere they go to feel recharged—their bedroom, the beach, that one park bench where you always seem to end up when you want to clear your head. Why not say "thank you" to a place that stands out to you, be it your garden or even the local laundromat.

fellow stain fighters
chorus of silent folding
all in this as one

Unfinished Business

Everyone has something in their life that they look back at and think, *damn*. Maybe it is a mistake you made, a friendship that fell apart, or something you wanted to say but never got the chance. Maybe it's someone who you always wanted to fight but you didn't have the guts. Think of just one instance that could use a do-over—whether it is a real possibility or not, it just might feel good to air it out here.

For the Scone Girl

one day I'll admit
how I read your diary
then asked you to move

70

Haiku for Less

What is something you want less of in your life?

bear trap in the woods
jealousy grips my ankle
but I hold the key

71

Haiku for Hope

Some say that hope is the
prediction of love in the future.
Others say hope is a passive
waste of active time. What does
hopefulness look like to you
right now, at this moment? Is
it the tiny chance of getting
back something you lost? Is it
improvement of your life? Strides
for the world at large? Is it active
or passive?

when the words come out
will they read as what they say?
hands clasped but arms wide

DATE: ___ • ___ • ___

72

Haiku for
Impending Doom

You just found out you're going to
die in a catastrophic event. But,
you can leave a haiku message
for the aliens invading. What,
dear reader, will you say?

take care of the plants
if they ever decide to
let you breathe again

DATE: ___ • ___ • ___

73.

Life Hack

Today, think of something that is irking you right now. You will be surprised how cathartic it can be to identify something, call it out, and commemorate it with a small poem.

if everyone drove
the way folks walk in New York
we would all be dead

DATE: ___ • ___ • ___

Haiku Pickup Line

Go to a public place—anywhere
with friendly strangers. Now,
think of an interesting opening
line for a haiku, and write it
below. It can be observational,
a set-up for a joke, a quote you
love. The more obscure and open-
ended the better. Next, find a
stranger that you'd like to meet.
Go up to them and say, "Pardon
me, but I'm halfway through
a haiku and I'd love for you to
finish it—want to give it a shot?"

over this ocean
I'd rather hang with you, bae

_____

_____

_____

DATE: ___ • ___ • ___

Haunted Haiku

When we were kids, we all loved playing Clue, telling ghost stories, reading *Goosebumps* books, and watching scary movies. When was the last time you thought up something good and creepy? Write it here, if you dare. . .

the rasp of cold breath
caressed the back of your neck
but you saw no one

76

Baby Crying Haiku

You hear it on the plane, at the restaurant, and even in the movies—babies crying everywhere. Your primal reaction is probably not particularly positive. We were all babies once, and the parent of this child is not happy either. It's the way it is, but share your thoughts in haiku.

no thanks, maitre'd!
we hardly mind waiting for
another table

Sonic Beauty

Some words seem more beautiful than others. What words have always piqued your ears? Mark Twain said the most beautiful phrase in the English language was "cellar door." Do you like particular letters, descriptors, or sounds, and have no idea why? Write a list of a few random words that sound beautiful to you, mull them over, and connect them into a haiku that could be total nonsense, but will surely sound like silk.

cunning / moonlight / catalyst /
surreptitious / august / seaworthy /
citrus / chartreuse / fox

she, a chartreuse fox
plucked the moonlight from the trees
like cunning citrus

DATE: ___ • ___ • ___

78

Give Props to What's Propping You Up

Stop right now. What is holding up this book? A table, your hand, your lap on the subway, the back of a sleeping dog on the couch? Whatever it is, appreciate for a moment the subtle and silent action of support for this book, for your whole environment. Give a little thanks below.

ah, turn the table
to straddle between my legs—
I don't have to lean

DATE: ___ • ___ • ___

79

Your Autobiography
Till Now

The power of the haiku comes
from its succinct and evocative
nature, so don't hold yourself
to a strictly linear or narrative
structure. You might start by
writing one sentence on your
childhood, young life, and
adulthood, or writing about
three of your most formative
experiences. Then, start pulling
out the most crucial words or
phrases and working them
together. You might be surprised
how profound your autobiography
can become, distilled to
seventeen syllables.

still I find myself
wanting to grow out my hair
and ride bikes all day

80

Haiku for More

What do you want more of? Get it,
starting here.

elderflower juice
it's full of vitamin C
an everyday treat

81

Haters Gonna Hate, Hate, Hate Haiku

A wise person once told us that negativity and hating are usually just manifestations of jealousy. If you've ever been hated on, that's probably the truth for you, too. Write yourself a badass haiku to remind yourself how to ignore the haters.

hatin' just a sign
somebody wanna be you—
they fear your glory

_____

_____

_____

DATE: ___ • ___ • ___

82

Haiku Yourself into Another Era

Have you ever pictured yourself living in another era? Prehistoric times roaming with dinosaurs, ancient Greece on the agora, Paris in the 1920s, or has some other time captured your imagination? Write yourself into that period, with all your senses.

my top hat got stuck
in almost every doorway
wooden wagon wheels

DATE: ___ • ___ • ___

83

Haiku for Your Hero

This is a haiku to appreciate
someone who inspires you, has
helped make you who you are, or
who gives you some other unique
support or momentum. Is it your
grandma who taught you to cook,
a historic figure you emulate,
or your best friend? Write their
name below, storm up a few
descriptors of them, maybe even
pull some quotes, and put them
together in a haiku shrine. If you
feel like it, share it with them, too.

Haiku for Gertrude Stein

you would never mind
right ideas or write orders
you push their buttons

DATE: ___ • ___ • ___

Senryu? Sen Ryu Who? Haiku

Senryu are basically the ancient Japanese equivalent of one-liner jokes. The power of humor is great, and when used correctly it can make even the simplest ideas more compelling and memorable. You can really challenge yourself by coming up with something totally unique, or go with something inspired by your favorite comedian.

Inspired by Mitch Hedberg

sometimes I wish that
I had an infestation
of koala bears

DATE: ___ • ___ • ___

Your Most Beloved Animal

Who loves you most? Who's a good boy? Who's the cutest little something something? We get asked to write haiku for pets all the time, and we know why: They are the biggest source of joy in so many of our human lives. Your pet probably can't read (or can they?) but we're pretty sure you'll still get a kick out of haikuing for them. Here's a haiku about a pair of enormous, blonde labradoodles.

when I wish that I
lived in a buffalo herd
I realize I do

DATE: ___ • ___ • ___

86

The Microscopic Ecosystem of the Teeny Tiny Poem

Look at the room or space around you as if it's a big bubble surrounding you. Now, shrink yourself down to the size of a paramecium. Take on its perspective and haiku about your tiny vast bubble of a universe.

dust hoping the door
lets another hurricane
sweep us off our feet

87

Eat That Fruit

Before you write today's haiku,
you need a piece of fruit. Set it on
the table and look at it. Pick it up.
Turn it over in your hands, feel
the weight, the texture. Is it soft
and vulnerable like a strawberry,
or protected by a tough skin?
Close your eyes and smell it.
Imagine how it will change when
you peel it, cut it, bite into it. . .
Think about the fruit's origin,
history, representation in culture,
and nutritional content. Love that
little fruit.
EAT. THAT. FRUIT.
Now, write a haiku.

teeth stuck full of guts
skin stings under fingernails
spit tangerine seeds

88

Haiku for a Revival

If you could revive anything, what would it be? Would you bring back bell-bottoms? Reinstate traditional courtship? Bring back to life your favorite childhood pet? You have the power to revive anything, but just one thing, so choose wisely.

so simple really
just a bedsheet wrapped 'round you—
togas back in style

DATE: ___ • ___ • ___

Two Words Collide

Think of two words, related in some specific way but distinct from each other. Write a haiku that could be a sneaky way of connecting these two words, but doesn't totally give away their association. Now for the real test: Tell your haiku to someone nearby, and see if they can venture a guess as to the words you are linking. Give them a chance to test you, too.

directions doze off
dancing on this disco ball
sunrise where sun sets

90

Haiku for Loneliness

What does loneliness feel like to you? When do you notice it? What helps you move through it?

corner of my eye
in the place where you once sat—
glad I bought a cat

91

Au Naturel

It's easy to forget about the natural world when you live in a town or city. But, ignoring nature just hurts its feelings. Go outside right now, and find something alive and growing. It can be a tree, some grass, or even a squirrel. Get as close to that living thing as you possibly can, and say, "Hey, I just want you to know I appreciate you. You look great today." Now, write a haiku about what it might say back.

*Bonus if you write this haiku naked!

thank you very much
for your shoes left at the door
blades of grass don't cut

92

Timelessness

Eckhart Tolle, known by some as the number one most spiritually influential person in the world, says that there is no time, there is only "The Now," and that time is a construct of our minds. What if, suddenly, you were able to stop time from passing, and exist only in this very moment? What would happen?

studying physics
in a book my head is down
then I look around

93

The Danger Zone

What is the most dangerous thing you've ever done? Was it a survival situation? A dare? Something you didn't even realize was dangerous at that moment? Would you do it again? Haiku it out.

sprinting as the train
pulling into its station
catching the first car

The Freudian Haiku

According to Sigmund Freud, our psyche is made up of three parts. The id is the primitive and instinctive component of personality. The ego makes decisions and makes sense of the real world. The superego is the morals, goals, and consciousness of the ideal self. Write a haiku with one line dedicated to each level of the psyche—what do you discover?

just a sip of wine
the bottle is open now. . .
should we finish it?

95

A Brand New Country

We celebrate the birth of our country every year, but what does it really mean for a nation to have its first moment of independence? If you could start your own free and independent land of _____, what would its haiku national anthem be? Declare it here.

this land is your land
everyone has their own land
and basic income

96

Baby, Make it Hurt So Good

We all experience pain—physical, emotional, spiritual, or some combination of all three. Often we're compelled to want to just take an aspirin or wish it away. But what if we could work with our pain, turn it into a person with whom we could have a conversation, hold hands, and walk together? What is a pain point in your life, and how can you personify it and walk with it, hand-in-hand?

hello, my old friend
I heard you have a lesson
to teach me today

It's the New Sensation

Write a haiku, anything you want, but write it backwards and with your non-dominant hand. Crazy, right? We know. Leonardo da Vinci loved doing stuff like this.

Leonardo knew
if you want to keep secrets
swallow your mirrors

DATE: ___ • ___ • ___

98

What is the Metaphor for Haiku?

A metaphor is a figure of speech. Some lucky word or phrase gets applied to another object or action to which it is not literally "applicable." Basically a metaphor can become a magical symbol that can become something else. Think up a scenario in your daily life, and convert it into a metaphor. Now, give that metaphor a haiku of its own—you may be surprised by just how applicable it is to the real situation.

all outta places
for both my eyes to wander
on long subway ride

DATE: ___ • ___ • ___

I Always Feel Like
Somebody's Watching Me

Using different characters
in writing is a great way to
explore thoughts and feelings
while getting out of our own
heads. Step outside yourself for
a moment and write a haiku
from the perspective of someone
observing you wherever you are
right now.

only the coffee
steam feels inspired. he looks to
the cat for some help

100

Haiku for Joy

What is something that makes you so happy you could burst? Go with your first instinct here.

first grape of the bunch
perfectly crisp and juicy—
pick of the litter

101

Completion in the End

What does it look like to finish something completely? Is it leaving something with no regrets? Or maybe it's a brief moment in a constantly evolving cycle of creation and destruction and recreation. Think for a moment about the phenomenon of completion and endings, and haiku it here.

any reckless heart
will understand the fact that
I love you to death

102

Haiku for the Meaning of Life

No big deal, right? Wrong. You're coming to the end of this book pretty soon here, and you should have figured it out by now. If you still aren't sure, mull it over today and feel free to look up words of wisdom on the theme from some of your favorite thinkers. Googling "what is the meaning of life" is always exciting. Then, write it out.

it has got to be
to write poems for as many
people as we can

DATE: ___ • ___ • ___

Haiku for the End of The World

Well, you did it. 102 Haiku. We're proud that you joined us on this journey and you should be, too.

Maybe you completed every haiku in one sitting. That's determination. Maybe you started this book two years ago and lost it and now a stranger is learning haiku. Sharing is caring. Perhaps you read this in reverse order, and just found out all of your poems are missing two syllables. If so, please contact our publisher and we will have a new book sent to you, free of charge.

No matter how you used this book, you've probably had some adventures with it. Now take that experience and apply it to your world in some way; let this be the beginning, not the end.

the apocalypse
could come at any moment—
so love even more

DATE: ___ • ___ • ___

Credits

Acknowledgements

We'd like to thank deeply our parents, our teachers, mentors, and friends, anyone who ever told us you can't make a business out of writing haiku on typewriters for people at parties, and every dog we've ever known. Also, special loving thanks to Jeff, Sean and Schuyler, the founders of Wanderlust, for discovering us in Brooklyn and inviting us to be a part of your festival. Huge gratitude to all the haiku guys and gals who have written with us and helped us grow: Tania Asnes, Peter Tiso, Micah Greenberg, Catalina Lavalle, Brandon Jordan Brown, Daniel Hoopes, Deena Hyatt, Mikumari Caiyhe, Scott Raven Tarazevits, Anthony McPherson, Peter Hornung, Andrew Bucket, Christoph Jenkins, Katharine Stockrahm, Victor Diaz Zapanta, Courtney McKenna, Katya Stepanova, Paasha Motamedi, Ian Pala, Mike Long, Logan Hollow, Chris Keener, Leah Clancy, Katya Stepanova, Lex Paulson, and probably a couple more we're missing.

We'd also like to thank all of the people for whom we've ever written, and each one of you for whom we have yet to write a poem. You're the reason we keep writing every single day.

answer to haiku 89: east / west